# UNDER THE
## pearl moon

*poems*

*r i c k   m a x s o n*

*ts* T. S. Poetry Press • New York

T. S. Poetry Press
Ossining, New York
Tspoetry.com

ISBN 978-1-943120-66-6
Cover photo by jack b., unsplash.com/@nervum

Maxson, Rick
  [Poems.]
  Under the Pearl Moon: Poems/Rick Maxson
  978-1-943120-66-6

A Second Opinion; Diamond; The Window-Maker's Shoes; Fortress;
The Vessel On My Uncle's Arm; Of Hat and Shoes; Mud Cat;
October Bones (Double Reverse Acrostic); Kiln; The Locust Tree;
Spring; Where I Went; Trying to Remember Florida; You Know This
Story; Heirloom; Hansel Alone; My European Education; her lace;
Pinot Noir; Saffron; Pilgrimage; The Decay of Volume One; Alice
Goes Underground; Refrigerator; Monster; Before the Rain; Tree Frog;
Photograph of a Poem; Moonlight Sonata; Horse Sense; Who Stole the
Tarts?; Leaving Carolina; Even When; Grounded; Stopping By the
Farming Pavilion; On Treasure Island; What I Share with the Rain;
Fortunes; SRV in the Parking Lot At the Quick Stop; Slipper; After
Dreams; Wedding Wish; Hearts; Window; Still Life; Mirror; A Kind of
Sleep first appeared on Tweetspeakpoetry.com. The Sirens and Please
Stay also appeared in *How To Write a Form Poem* by Tania Runyan. Birds
in Home Depot—December also appeared in *Earth Song: A Nature Poems
Experience,* editor Sara Barkat, and in The Poetry Foundation's podcast
The Slowdown. SRV in the Parking Lot At the Quick Stop also
appeared in *How To Read a Poem* by Tania Runyan.

*for carol, allison and abby*

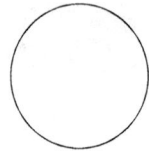

# CONTENTS

## Eno

Let it be the river Eno—
as if the map of where is wind,
it buckles in the autumn trees and grasses.
Back bent on a lift of limb
I twist, as sap drops like alluvium scattered
on steep slopes, where water weakened in its course.
I would so quietly live
among the particles of light and air, a hue
ubiquitously hiding along guiding banks of green,
garden, rake, and furrow,
yellow aging tear-shape falling,
wet and taken, leaf and ribbon…

# I • Ohio

In 1947 my mother and my aunt Mable bought a Craftsman style duplex for $10,000 in the north end of Columbus, Ohio, on Medary Avenue. The street's umber blocks, each stamped with Nelsonville Block, were laid one-by-one in the late 1890s. It was my good fortune to live next door to my uncle Jack, who possessed everything I would need from a male figure in my early growing years. Retired from the Marine Corps, he taught me skills that remain with me a lifetime later. Mabel was the assistant to the Comptroller of the City of Columbus. She was refined and quiet, the opposite of Jack, boisterous, and at times crude. On his right arm was a tattoo, a very close likeness of Mabel. On his left arm a Marines symbol of an eagle with the world in its talons. For his rough ways, Jack was kind and capable of tremendous gentleness and respect for all things living.

At the back of that duplex, my father descended six concrete stairs each morning, where he made art glass, mostly for church windows around the city of Columbus, and as far north as Sandusky, and to the south as far as Cincinnati and Portsmouth. That small workshop was full of sounds and images: his boot steps and shuffling on the concrete floor as he rounded the work table assembling windows with lead and solder, forming the halos of saints and the wings of angels; the shelves of glass sheets; the small heater in winter; and the fine glass dust on the floor, swept from the table and rendered harmless. My father was fierce and strict, as much as he held a hidden kindness that I seldom recognized. He was there when I opened my eyes from unconsciousness, falling from trees; in an ambulance when I was hit by a car. As he lay in repose at his funeral, I remember placing my hand on his heart, perhaps the closest emotionally I ever came to him. He was an artist. It took me years to understand him.

Medary was the only remaining brick street of those I travelled, on my stripped down, green Schwinn. A slow and sturdy surface that received the energy of our shouts each morning as we set out toward the schools, or began our weekend adventures. Every evening, under the street lamps, the bricks seemed to hold us in their glazed glow until porch lights flickered and the doorways of each house opened with the first calls for us to come home.

What enhanced the breadth and magic of that province was the labyrinth of gravel alleyways that laced the streets in all directions. Gray and dusty veins loomed along the garages that held the tantalizing and forgotten junk of adult life, the trinkets, toys and taboo magazines that verified or vilified the veneer of decorum by which we all knew our parents. We knew these passages by their position in the network of streets, whose house they bordered, or their function within our daily meanderings. There were fields along the streets and alleys where we would build forts from tree and lumber scraps. In these precarious shelters, we would eat Mr. Anderton's concord grapes and smoke the dried grapevines like cigarettes as we discussed girls, our prowess with our bicycles, the eccentrics of the neighborhood. The fields were riddled with brambles and berries, steep banks, the detritus of occasional midnight dumps from trucks never seen. We spent many summer days climbing the large green apple tree in the field along Clinton Street, getting stomach aches from its fruit. The fields were the theaters of indelible events in our lives. Next to the apple tree was an old large house, boarded up with signs of *Danger!* and *No Trespassing!* Of course, we explored it from basement to attic, while reciting stories we claimed to have heard about former residents.

Clinton Street was essentially the heart of the neighborhood harboring the fear and joy of boys discovering the infinitesimal elements that would define them as they grew. One of the most exhilarating times was during the winter snows. For our pleasure, the city of Columbus would block off Clinton in every direction so we could experience the swift acceleration of its incline on sleds, homemade or purchased. Mine was a Flexible Flyer I bought with money I earned collecting pop bottles and coat hangers from the neighbors.

Medary remains an old, seemingly isolated street lined with Craftsman duplexes. The alleys are still there, but the gravel surfaces are now paved, as is the brick street. The Locust tree between the front yards of our house and Slocomb's is a stump. In our backyard, the trunk of the Elm is a chopping block five feet in diameter. The stone garage, my father's workshop, is gone. The little field across that alley has been leveled ten feet and is filled with single story apartments, where a grape arbor once stood.

## A Second Opinion

Some scars are not closures,
they want something
to be made of them, a door,
or a vine; this scar
on my ankle, climbing
the remainder of my life, giving
direction to desire.

We all want this,
a beanstalk to the clouds,
the skin as a map—constant,
easy to fold—
the bend in the road
obscuring the glare
of what we were.

Today the locusts started
their saws singing
and this evening
one left its mask clinging
to the furrows of a cottonwood.

As children we wore their forsaken shells—
grim face, fishhook legs—
a brittle pouch for hopeless
and misunderstood longings.
For years my body has been the husk
of something moving inside,

balanced on a thread
high above my life,
while I strained to see
of what the thread was made.

# Diamond

The diamond disk cuts,
leaves a fine dust veed
along the strike-line
tapped to break the glass.

On the floor,
in your workshop
I played,
brushing together what fell
as your boots moved,
speckled with solder stars.

Light reflected off
the bright grains, where
it fell, in a memory of sand.

It was harmless in my hand,
edge dissolved by edge,
a child's slightest sigh sent it
spiraling like a galaxy.

Such weightless days
rescue years,
like dust and starlight.

## The Window-Maker's Shoes

*for Richard Clayton Maxson (1922-2006)*

Shoes speckled with stars
from solder, fallen.
Paint and putty where he walked
among the racks of glass, studio garage
I swept to help; shoes with winters
in their folds, haunting
the chambers of his now;
the sound of shuffling—soft,
as he went around the tables
as he tapped and sealed lead against the joins;
sounds living for a moment, each one
disappearing into the next,
then each one gone.

## Fortress

To that darkness beneath
Autumn after Autumn,

beneath the Elm leaves
pushed to the back of the yard

by winds you knew sufficiently
to name, by small, unnoticed breezes,

I came to hear my breathing,
a chamber in a chamber

that magnified me quietly
within its humid echo,

gave me presence,
like the hungry scuffling of squirrels—

each memory a wound,
each leaf that fell, a touch.

## The Vessel On My Uncle's Arm

Its mysterious script,
gun-barrel-blue, moving
as he steered the fragile spokes
of my small hand while the locomotive
moved forward like a planet
yawing into the roundhouse.
The gear sounds, jangle and prang
of steel, were the winds I saw
pushing against the sails,
the curl of the bow wave
as the sea reclaimed it, two ships,
iron and ink, that moved me along,
engines turning engines.
He is still with me, blue skin
of sail, artful vein
running through my life. It renders
the shadows of the moon, and storms,
brings the Sun Boat at daybreak.
From the fine lines of its prow,
how stalwart are
the weightless birds at feeders
in the steel of winter; I see mountains
scored and rising over trackshine,
in a sea of sky,
where clouds of sparrows turn like serifs.

## Of Hat and Shoes

Should I remove my shoes?
In her wimple, kneeling on the floor,
Sister Cecilia's rhythm caught my ear,

and only then my eye, her sleeves rolled,
her arms dimpling with the strain,
the sound of winter pines rubbing in the wind,
caught in her song and scrubbing.

Should I touch my hat,
passing her on the narrow stairs—a breeze
follows her habit of Poor Clares—the brim
across my stare, do I dare to raise my hand?

How is it those trees are more beautiful in snow
against their hidden seeds and wrap of bark?

How shall I confess these reveries, and less
than that, what becomes of love not blessed?

# Mud Cat

A fish so still unnerved them,
devouring sixty inches of their minds:
this was the mighty Muskingum
cataract, falling no further
than half a mile upstream.

A small hope, shared by many: after
the flood of Fifty—they'd find it
moved. Yet, when a month of mud
cleared, it seemed only fatter than before,
near the dock where the cattails clatter.

Some swore through time, red-faced,
it was a keelhauled bow they saw,
something sunk and bogged down,
sucked-in so much the river that plucked
off seven bridges like steel flowers left it placed.

Swearing came to dares for feats
and fears of wrestling with the beast.
Wives were taxed for recipes of blood
and dough and meats, yet through years
of snarls and snells, the monster would not eat.

One morning it was gone, and took its lore.
The mooring dried and shriveled,
wobbled on its legs, and stories,
shifted to the past like chum, tried
luring back the fish, and languid lingered:

their thoughts beyond the cast, the fish got none:
how the river unseen sifted through its
solitary heart and why, one night,
as with elusive poems and dreams,
it raised its dorsal mast and drifted on.

## October Bones

*Double Reverse Acrostic*

Counting failed always, the first gleaming eye
Of a fox or coon, screech owl, or deer scream
Raised the hair on my neck and stopped me. I
Never failed to fear those yellow eyes; that
Fear was the reason as a child—the moon
Inches from the earth—yellow at first, as if I
Envisioned what was to come—I came. A ghost,
Later in the sky, the moon rendered the stalks
Dead like bones, an eerie light, but I would go
Slowly, over furrows, row by row, as not to fall.

# Kiln

Regardless, I am there,
where you are the glass.
You have always been
exalted, high in a holy place,
forbidden in whispers,
knelt beneath,
illuminated through masks.

And there was the kiln:
under the basement stairs,
the glow in plunder orange,
the pliant you, abstracted,
your walk far from your hands
in prayer, the slag —
scoria and clinker of process,
ruin of dogma —
the father's father's father's father,
world without end,     all linked
in the heavy, impenetrable density of lead.

Nevertheless, I am here
in a white glow, an ordinary night,
with these fragments, fragile as glass,
and I think, why do I write your poem
over and over; how is it I see you
broken and scattered in my head—
smallest, brightest, dancing flowers,
greenest, deepest-bowing blades of grass.

# The Locust Tree

Its winter branches assembled the sky
into jigsaw pieces, worn and gray,
a winding sheet caught on its thorns,
dropped over housetops and chimneys
spilling ash on heaps of snow.

We watched the ants moil over oozing sap
from roots that rose into a split
trunk that sent fissures into the air,
a black crack that abducted our attention,
its brittle castings clinging,
splitting walkways, driving them upward
like headlands rising at a sea's edge.

It cut us when we stumbled
on the concrete, rough shingles of bark
like concertina wire.

When the parents set the boys free
to play over the brick streets,
it was there,
penumbra of night.

In an old garage,
void of any light,
we spoke as locusts do,
and shed our child-masks.
Our cigarettes pulsed
their slow fiery hearts;

we droned our stories,
drawn smoke-husky, thorn-caught
into the alleyways away from home.

## II • Florida

We hadn't been to Florida since I was seven or eight years old. I didn't know why. There were family pressures my sister and I could feel, but aside from the audible arguments between our parents, behind closed doors, and occasionally the strained air of verbal exchanges in the car we knew nothing about our parents' lives. I was in the seventh grade, my sister, Janet, in fourth. We were close until I grew into the reclusiveness that would define my nature. I thought my need to be alone was a defense, a shield from the differences I felt between my family's way of life, my teachers' dogmatic views, and the insecurities of my peers that propelled them to ridicule those who were shy, clumsy, foreign, or had any mark of distinction other than their own. In spite of how we began as brother and sister, we shared the same early sense of humor, playful invention, and adventure.

In the final months of my mother's pregnancy with Janet, I was put on a train with my aunt Bessie, to Kentucky from Ohio, until after Janet was born. I had never met nor heard about my aunt, her husband Ed, nor their two daughters Donna and Judy. There are events in life that bury themselves deep in our souls, affecting us with subtle force to respond to the world in ways that leave us forever puzzled with that response. This was one of those events. I don't remember it except that it was raining, I was crying, my mother was crying, and Bessie said it was because my father would not buy my mother ice cream. The station slowly moved away from me, and for months I lived uncomfortably with the Lynd family. My only comfort there was their farm. I played in the barn with Donna and Judy when they were home from school. I suffered their teasing, and their occasional aloofness. When I returned home I had a baby sister.

My brothers, Billy and Eddie, were born years later in Columbus. As a kid, I did not excel at anything. The height of my grade school athletic prowess came with hitting a grand-slam during a lunch hour softball game when I was ten. As I made my way to resume class, amid pats on the back and unfamiliar congratulations, my father appeared and pulled me out of that joy to say, "You have a new baby brother." I seemed torn between two worlds: one I had just entered, never having been there before among my peers, and one I only knew from hearing how joyful it should be.

In the early 1950s, we drove each year through the treacherous mountain roads of North Carolina to Florida in my father's Willys Jeep, always stopping at the Mount Airy Motel, where Janet and I would swim in the pool in the evening until our lips turned blue. It may have been these trips that made me fall in love with mountains, the freshness they gave to the cool air, and the fog that seemed ever present, especially in mornings. Driving through them, I loved the tortuous windings, the precipitous drops with no guard rails, so that the tree tops below loomed off the road edge as though we were flying. Along the cliffs rising over the left of the road, water frequently ran in rivulets over the granite's jagged surface where the mountain was chiseled away. Occasionally we stopped at the overlooks contrary to my begging to stop at every one. I took deep breaths there, some of which I believe still remain inside me.

That my grandfather lived in Florida was the initial best part about moving there. Tom Morris was a redeeming mystery. He stood six-foot-four and was well into his sixties when I first encountered him. He lived with Helen, his second wife, both devout believers, evident for her in the tranquility of her quilt making and knitting, he in television evangelists, like Oral Roberts and Kathryn Kuhlman, who drained my grandfather of thousands of dollars. He sat for hours, with his parakeet Sweety, watching these preachers on TV. He would place his hand, as instructed, on the TV screen and pray, for what I did not know.

Florida had a fragrance—salt air, for sure—but something else musty, earthy. I have never adequately described it in my mind. My grandfather's house seemed to be the flower that disseminated it. When I was there I was at the center of the bloom. The scent was in his backyard filled with avocado, grapefruit, orange, kumquat, and banana trees. Beyond that seeming forest lay his garage and the apartment above it, where I was allowed to sleep at night alone, the jalousie windows cranked open to let in the sounds of owls and whippoorwills, and the redolence that was the night.

I adored my grandfather, his strength, his seeming knowledge of everything. He was a mechanic in his younger years and had invented an early model of a coin operated washing machine. He owned a laundromat and many houses that he rented in Ormond Beach and Daytona Beach. When I was eight years old he took me for the first time fishing on the Saint John's River. It was March and the Crappie were spawning. We fished with cane poles and caught dozens we kept in a live well. The fishing was thrilling, but it was rivaled by seeing the wild boar pacing on the shoreline, angry at our proximity. And at night hearing the panthers cry. "It's just a panther," my grandpa would say, "they won't come near the cabins. The cabins were nothing more than four walls around an open area and a bathroom. Around the top of the walls an eighteen inch screen surrounded the cabin against mosquitoes. One morning at the boat dock I saw my grandpa reach up and grab a copperhead snake with one hand and swing it against a post to kill it. There were stories at the docks about alligators and lost hands from those who naively let one drag along the boat in the cool water. I was never frightened. I felt protected. Feeling protected was not something I felt at home. It was a distant land from this wild and exciting world, a gulf apart, along the meandering waters of a river that showed me grassy wetland, swampy marshlands filled with the darkened roots of cypress trees, birds—herons, egrets, blackbirds, osprey, and kingfishers. I felt most at home in the wild, and I remained so all through the adult years I spent in Florida.

Hurricane Carla hit Houston, Texas, in 1961 and my father moved to Houston at the behest of Pittsburgh Plate Glass company, his employer then, to help replace the windows blown out of high rise office buildings. He would call home and tell us about the rattlesnakes loose in the streets slithering amidst the wreckage. After several weeks my mother sold our house in Florida and we moved to Houston in June and rented a house with no air conditioning. We slept with a fan. In Columbus, John Green was the only regional accent I had ever encountered. In Houston everyone had a drawl. Two-syllable words were converted by it to three syllables. Just one month later, my mother gathered the family in the living room and asked, "Would you rather have new furniture, or move to Spain?" The question was astonishing to say the least, and delivered almost rhetorically. My mother always seemed to get whatever she wanted. Spain won out and she began selling everything we owned that survived the move from Florida: pictures off the walls, our dinnerware and flatware, cookware, rugs, even the family car. My father quit his job as a glazer. We could hear him crying late at night as he and my mother argued. She would curse him, tell him to shut up and quit crying.

In Florida, during my father's absence my mother met a man named Vincent. He lived with his sister and her two daughters, Maria and Amparo. They were from Madrid, Spain. Vincent was erudite, and for my mother charismatic, worldly, and effusive. While my father was working in Houston we went to Vincent's house for dinner, where he filled her head with the riches ostensibly available in Spain, and the possibility of my father "apprenticing" under the Spanish stained-glass masters, like those working on Sagrada Familia in Barcelona, the still unfinished cathedral designed and begun by Antoni Gaudi in 1882. None of Vincent's promises achieved a reality for our family. They merely fed my mother's desire for us to be something we were not.

## Spring

Scattered far, the gray horses
of my yearning, the way horses

galloping are free from the earth
for a moment. We can't say horses

fly though. Can't say those plumed seeds
will bloom bright, when April horses

on their illusive wings run wild
across my wishes where they lay, horses

that kick and splay the rick of wood,
with spring abandon, as is the way of horses.

## Where I Went

In the tops of trees, swayed
into the countryside of dreams,
on waves of air, I was lost and found,
high above browned grasses.
The tartan of rooftops
lay harmless below me
as I flew, a nameless bird
over the broken concrete walks
that burned my feet, now far
from the spines of the locust tree,
over the canals lined with old men
fishing for eels, in the cattails.
I circled in a wind from somewhere
and I was all the noises no one silenced,
open like the hope in suffering,
open like a bell in gray light.
There, on a spindle of leaves,
I watched the birds aloft
on the vapor of their wings
and I flew for hours not knowing where.

# Trying to Remember Florida

A sad fable unfolds:

Fear has left its song in the air,
heavy with disaster and

the snakes coil artfully,
rising from patio tables
in bird cages that keep us safe.

The whirlpool is strongest here,
cut from the sky,
pieces of starless, moonless night,
hang out at the car wash
and the schoolyards.

Florida, fragrance
in my youth.

From our home
there was a calculus of roads
that led from true north,
an expectation
written into the simple lines
of mountain lanes
that twisted and terrified
the unbaptized.

Dismal diary of rust
crumbling in memory, trees
bent in the wind's wake,
veil of moss on live oaks,
the vanishing we failed to see

## You Know This Story

*for Janet*

In the story I tell that begins with you,
there is a dark hallway with chairs,
and the solid beams of flashlights,
like brilliant roads leading
to your laughing heart.

To the casual reader,
dark hallways are scary,
but then this is the flashlight's
adult end, with sharp edges.

Where you are, the light is soft
and wide, in a forest of chair legs,
a sky of bed sheets, as far away
as I can see from the here and now.

What is now would have been mysterious,
like a journey to a foreign land,
you in the light of children,
so far from make believe, doing work
you would not have imagined.

Sometimes there is a small door
in the distance of a memory,
a slice through the riddle of time.
There waits a sound, a thought,
a secret to be kept beyond reason.

You know this story:
Mount Airy, where the Willys stopped,
half way to Florida; we swam
until our teeth chattered, in the frail air,
the lavender shoulders in the distance,
enduring the ages of the vaulted stars;
you must remember, the water was so warm.

Even after we were gone, the water,
unnoticed from the here and now,
continues gathering the day's warmth
and each night holds it until morning,
for the someday we might return.

# Heirloom

*for Helen*

The fine lace fallen
from your knees,
the story of your quiet life,
in the rhythmic clicking
of the points
the circling needle heads
your gravel voice,
like fish roe frying,
a church fan folded
near the knitting chair,
the hands of weather gauges
and the clock,
moving slowly on the wall,
as the palm-pressed prayers
living in your freckled hands,
moved into these knots, these threads.

## Hansel Alone

The trees leaned,
the storm lost in memory;
rain-troughed clay streets
stopped and a sand path
began its turn into the woods
like a hag's cough.

Once a sweeter voice
beckoned me into the yellow pines,
the gnarled fingers of the oaks
with their moss shawls.

As if I could return,
and once again be lost in those woods,
I stared from my car at the houses,
and the street sign that must be wrong.

Nothing sinister remained
behind the yards, behind coral and lime walls,
no path led back from where I came
and no friend met me.

This is the fate of fables,
muted in a thin brake,
rimmed in pastel houses.

I turned toward town, remembering
the way bicycles bounced us
like jackhammers, over the furrowed

clay streets making chants
from the vowels of our laughter.

The trees along River Rd. opened to the city.
Over the Halifax River the old draw bridge
and pylons were gone, replaced
by the high arch of a new bridge, no place,

for the gulls to perch. I watched them
circle, their bellies full of crumbs.

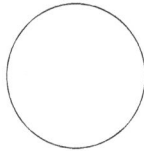

## III • Spain

I watched as a rat made its way up the docking rope in moon-
light. This was my first glimpse of New York City as I awoke in
the backseat of a car. The docking rope had more than ample
width that the creature's small feet needed to ascend to the SS
Independence that would take us to Spain. Neither my mother
nor father saw the rat, or if they did, they said nothing. It was
five o'clock in the morning. My father had driven all day for
three days from Houston. We were to meet Vincent Diaz later
that day, and we would all board the Independence together.
Beyond the great passenger ship and the wharf the sun was ris-
ing over the edge of a slick ocean on which we would soon be
sailing. I was fifteen, my sister twelve, Billy was five and my
youngest brother Eddie two. As children we were living in a mys-
tery fashioned by hapless adults going somewhere as dissimilar
to their dreams as the Atlantic and Pacific oceans. While my fa-
ther dreamed of his workshop back on Medary Ave. in Colum-
bus, Ohio, my mother's fantasy was her children having a
"European education," her husband an apprenticeship under
stain-glass masters in Barcelona, and perhaps even a romantic
tryst with a well-off, educated Spanish gentleman named Vin-
cent.

As strange and awkward as this excursion was, I also saw it
as an adventure. What was once mythic became real.  It took
nine days to cross the Atlantic. I spent my days exploring the
ship decks and playing games in the solarium. At night I would
sneak out of our cabin-class sleeping quarters to watch the water
as it leveled into a sheet of glass full of stars that met the sky on

the horizon and seemed to tumble over the edge, a bejeweled waterfall. There were the ports of call, Canary Islands, Morocco, Madeira. I remember being on deck when we approached Madeira one morning. It was cinematic, with gulls circling colossal cliffs fringed with puffs of cloud, the sun slowly pulling them apart into ribbons drifting into the rock and ocean below. The journey to Spain was like a nightmare that slipped in and out of an amazing dream. Those lapses into fancy will never leave me.

We rented a luxuriously furnished ten room apartment in Madrid. It came with a live-in maid named Gabi. The apartment was located on Paseo Del Prado across from the Prado museum. The avenue was broad with esplanades of large trees whose panniers met to form shaded tunnels towering over the walkways, where vendors of calamari and *helados* and balloons waited patiently and quietly for their ambling patrons. These arbors were interrupted by crowded roundabouts surrounding circular fountains, their mottled depths glistening with the wishes of visitors.

The apartment was one of two separated by a spacious courtyard of cobblestone. Our Spanish neighbors were an extended family, who often cooked paella on a large fire pit. We were invited to a few of these celebrations. Spaniards ate their evening meals at nine or ten o'clock, under the lights, under the starry skies. Their family would lay a hardwood section of flooring over the surface of a section of courtyard for flamenco dancers while the guitarist played and sang until the stars were well-risen.

My sister and I were both put in boarding schools. Janet's was run by Dominican nuns, mine by Franciscan monks. We were there seven days a week, allowed a home visit twice a month. Neither school contained anyone who spoke English. In retrospect, my adventurist spirit rescued me from the potential horror of this arrangement. Some parts were frightening—the swelling of my abdomen from strange food, the discipline of sashes across my legs (though not a stranger to me). Other parts were exhilarating—the Madrid subway, calamari sandwiches and beer, most of all Isabel, the calamari vendor's daughter, my guide and my friend. She spoke English and she laughed and infected me with it. We roamed over the streets of Madrid together. Saw the museums and cathedrals replete with paintings and statues that both awed and amused us. We sat on benches in the esplanades and plazas and laughed at the people bustling around us. For Janet, twelve years old, my mother's experiment for our family *was* a nightmare. Our parents never acknowledged what we might be going through. My father left months before us, crying as he boarded the plane, never the apprentice of my mother's dreams. Eventually, like all dreams, we awoke and returned to Columbus, Ohio, where I saw how some nightmares survive our awakening.

## The Sirens

*a found poem from Franz Kafka's "Parable and Paradox"*

These are the seductive voices
of the night; the Sirens too
sang that way.

It would be doing them an injustice
to think that they wanted
to seduce;

they knew they had claws and sterile
wombs, and they lamented
this aloud.

They could not help it
if their laments sounded so
beautiful.

## My European Education

Mother loved the Spanish gentleman,
his sapient ways, his voice that rolled
off the dark oils of Goya in Seville.

Altar to altar she followed him,
with her hollow prayers and sacrifices
broken from their lives like fruit from trees.

On the veranda she raised her demitasse:
to Granada, the Alhambra—her dream for us,
purged of the calloused and quotidian.

Along the esplanades she followed him,
gesturing to the ancient relief dropping tears
over the inspirited coins, its sanguine pool
quivering as she passed.

## her lace

the reason not at first for escape from the boarding of boys hoard-
ing of boys into lines with their sashes binding brown cassocks the
friars up all night patrolling the school for boys being boys after
lights out her lace after the first dark glance up from where so
deep it lay against her Spanish skin her hair slashing it like a
narrow brush stroke of the darkest lightning busy her father
calamari vendor saying yes to let her go the metro and her hand
not shy in mine that first day my heart like wheels on tracks her
lace so soft appearing memory blends the light off stone streets
and how the grand *brise soleil* of buildings so ancient to soften
the sun under their relief and us and paintings older than all
those who put us there forgetting the school and fathers and
friars her lace cut from abuela's dress and shaped under the
length of her neck the marble columns so soft in light the hands
before our hands as we rounded them against the cool how it
moved like air under silk when she spoke and laughed the soft
colors of her lace surfacing through years to then and now in my
aging of it further from that young girl and young man in
Madrid alone the way a reflection in a rain puddle is alone as the
street strides by and someone ripples it like the tatting surfacing
from the image of…

## Pinot Noir

Perhaps it is your color,
roses and blackberries,
or the warm nights—
the young vintner
in the field with his love,
the body's blush rising
into the dry air, flesh
ripe and taut beneath
the spare dress,
the press of skin—
Ah! the sighs, the aroma
of love, revealed
along my tongue, tasting
even moonlight.

## Saffron

From out of the cockled skirts,
the heels and castanets,
you found me,
your crimson threads,
the passion of guitars.

I might have been a wanderer,
the light, ascending flames,
Paseo del Prado,
Madrid transformed,
as evening did all things mortal:
beyond the courtyard,
collecting the esplanades
of great trees into forests,
the fountains into rivers.

Flower of the fall,
with your feast of flesh,
your gentle tongue on mine,
soft and lingering kiss,
my sultry Spanish dancer.

## Pilgrimage

To when would you go back if you could?
In the spring there may be snow
along the curbs, where time has hurried
on and failed to bring along the melting,
the way dreams are nothing more
than what lies beneath a life.

Dragons at the door of an old man's house,
one afternoon, no certain reason, a nap,
a lapse, a moment with a gift for gathering:

brass, lifeless dragons hissed, nonetheless,
on the table lisse—a magician he was,
quiet German, tool & die, brass spittoons,

unkempt rooms; a hue & cry against his youth,
the forty-eight displayed, dust and age,
the alchemist—silk-red to blood, hate to craft:

outside, the locust tree, the dark divide
from which I rose, and return to frequently,
its limbs of why and tangled stars,

the sky sat on its knee, twilight puppet
by branches dark moved, and Autumn's plague began
its aria, hymns from the choir sarcophagi.

Fifteen at Guernica, I burned the Prado
for a father, slept in its smoky arms.

## The Decay of Volume One

Ocherous binding, Volume I, long in waiting
for my return from the world of hours;
the dragons are old, the princess
sleeps on her gold gone gray.
Behind me is a precious time, a journey
unknown and inevitable, the dreaded bath
I must take, two lives like soap bubbles aloft
collision bound by a single breath.
Where are the rats who ate their tales,
the mice who blindly tattered pages
keeping the children lost, the jumbled spells
leaving the apples impaled on thorns.
The stories in pieces now, my fingers
struggling with pages of confetti
made from golden locks of hair,
the rag of a faded hood, a splintered basket.
The witches' words melt like flakes
of snow, only a bag of tricks now,
a cackle from a dark box, on a house
of crumbs, where lived a boy.
In a shadowed wood the years have made
from improbable things, buried
in the colors of October, I sit with a faded book
at a table disappearing at both ends

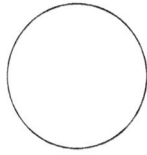

## IV • Ohio Again

Perhaps the return accommodations on Greenwich Street my father had arranged were too far from the castles in Spain in my mother's dreams. The three bedroom apartment rental was one of fifteen along a cement walk against a sparsely grassed common yard with swing sets and picnic tables behind the Northern Lights Shopping Center bowling alley. A tall wooden fence separated the apartments from the alley parking lot. All that remained visible to the residents were the words *bowling alley* in red neon, the *y* of which blinked and faded intermittently with a loud electric hiss. From beyond the fence, the shouts, the revving of hot cars, the swearing and frequent police sirens rose above the useless barricade and came shattering down into the narrow strip of lawn where the children played and the adults sat in the evenings at picnic tables scattered in semi-private distances, one for every three back doors.

A few weeks after our return to Columbus I awoke to my father's loud voice with intermittent slapping sounds. I followed these to my parents' bedroom. My mother was not awake and he was slapping her face. He ran to the phone and I walked in and sat on the edge of the bed. My mother turned her head toward me and said, "I don't want to live anymore" and then faded away. My father returned to trying to wake her, and soon after the room was filled with EMTs. We were all asked to leave the room. I went out into the compact hallway and put my seventeen year old fist through a closet door as I screamed, my sister behind me asking what was going on, my little brothers both crying at the mayhem filling our home.

My mother had saved Nembutal capsules my grandmother, a nurse, had given her for headaches. Elsie, my father's mother had no idea what she had been through, other than what my father related on his return to Columbus six months before us. Elsie followed us to the hospital where they pumped the residual drugs from my mother's stomach. In the days that followed my mother recovered, and was released, and contacted her children from a house in Reynoldsburg, a city not far from Columbus.

I began growing numb and attended high school bewildered and angry, disengaged from classes, sports, and even friendships. After school I hurried to my job at Harmony House, a record store in the nearby shopping center. There I felt needed and for a brief few hours I seemed to have a purpose. The store owner, Carl McFadden sought my advice about current music. It was 1964. The Beatles arrived in America around the same time as the Rolling Stones. Carl was enamored with the classics like Frank Sinatra. He said Elvis was the last of the great crooners. I learned responsibility without intimidation, pride without conceit. Even today I remember it as a threshold into adulthood that tempered the rowdiness I sought.

In the next interminable and strained few months, we learned our parents would be divorced and we would be living with our father behind the bowling alley, making the best of the life that seemed to be disintegrating before our eyes. Within that quagmire, my father met Anne. It was a pleasant transformation to see the change for the better in my father to be with a woman who actually loved him. They were married after about a year and bought a house on Dresden Street adjacent to the shopping center. The house had three bedrooms and one bathroom. Our families combined were two adults and seven children. It was not a happy place for me. My father became increasingly angry with me as I tried to extricate myself from the harshness of his discipline. When he insisted on feeding us cherry Jell-O® in liquid form, before it gelled, that it was the same as Kool-Aid®, and I told him he was wrong, he went to hit me with one hand. I stopped him. He raised the other hand to strike my face. I stopped him again. I held both his wrists in my hands and said, "No more."

After I graduated from Brookhaven High School, I was seldom home on Dresden St., working in a lumber yard during the day, and spending long hours dancing at Luv-a-Go-Go and drinking at Ben's Tavern across from Ohio State University. I bought a 1964 GTO, and with the help of the Sullivan brothers rebuilt the engine to racing class. For a while street racing, dancing, and drinking seemed fulfilling, but one morning I arrived at work to see a notice on the bulletin board:

> *Sutherland Lumber in Anaheim, CA*
> *has an opening for a salesman/loader.*
> *Experience reading house plans*
> *and figuring supplies. Pay rate TBD*

My application for the salesman/loader with Sutherland Lumber was approved, and I moved to California the following week to escape what seemed would be a grim existence living in my father's house. For a while I struggled with whether that was cruel that I left my sister and brothers, my friends without a thought. I was self-centered, selfish, and committed to any life other than what lay ruined and pointless behind me. Working in the lumber yard, I was depressed at first, but found changes happening with my attentions, my feelings for the world, and my willingness to take chances even more daring than my move, alone, so far from my place of birth. In a way I did not recognize myself, but in a way this severance registered as life-saving, reversing years of damage. It was a similar feeling, I recall now, as when I reversed the door with the hole in it I had made on Greenwich Street, buried it in the darkness of a closet I never used.

# Alice Goes Underground

...the winding of string leads nowhere.
The first end, buried deep in the wound
and circling years, is what we seek—

the true beginning—before gathering
shaped us, and our tale evaporated
in the telling of it, into scattered pinwheels

waiting for the wind to turn, the way
it moves the grass, or like water moving
in the sun as it gathers the light into color.

Begin with the heat on your back; the sun
bleaches the sand white you thought,
dry and fine for the crabs pulling

at the fragments of netting. Mother warned
it was too soft, too hot except for the caucus
of claws dragging the decaying web

into the hole, into the small darkness floating
in the white sand, where, you thought to go—
Follow the strands drawn behind them,

as they disappear deep into the dark wound.
You are a child then, all things are possible;
you don't think...

## Refrigerator

The refrigerator door, art's highest appreciation,
the ultimate publication for a child.
As close to food as words can come.
A poem unfettered by rationality, honored
to be here beneath its own magnet—a medal
pinned on a lapel. Stop here a moment—

listen to the humming, an engine,
the song inside full of crisp,
perishable notes that wither in the air,
the words lined up here, a dispensary
of indispensable details:

a jar of corrugated green pickles, an array
of headless shrimp, fiery maraschino cherries,
a fruit salad, veggie platter, assortments of
cheeses and chilled French wines, a pink
bottle of amoxicillin: the poem is infectious.

A celebration. The music, the revelry,
is seeping through the white door.

# Monster

*after Frankenstein*

Love was in the hopelessness of you,
each word a part of how you would be.

Imaginings have a way of forming themselves
from a wish for light, a wager to conceive a ghost.

This is how you were born from her, barely born herself.
You, created twice, a story and a story's child.

A god less knowing watched her write each page,
the glory and the fear that was your life,

rising out of her desire, rising from a myth
before her eyes, piece by piece, from dream to fire.

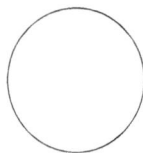

# V • California

Leaving Columbus, Ohio, to go to California was not a difficult decision. Working in a lumber yard wasn't something I wanted. The trouble was I didn't know what I wanted. Why California, I didn't know, other than it seemed so different than Ohio. Of course I was affected by many of the popular songs by The Beach Boys, the movies about beach parties, precocious girls, and fast cars. I traded my GTO on a Lemans the week I prepared for the drive. It was September. I spent a final night at Ben's Tavern and said goodbye to my friends before heading west. All I owned was in the trunk of my car: clothes, a dozen books, a few albums—Beatles, Beach Boys, and The Velvet Underground. I was leaving the life in which I had been raised, a winter that followed me from childhood and was coming for me once again.

When I reached the Ohio border and crossed into Indiana, the world seemed to open as if I could see all the way to Los Angeles. I was grinning and my heart was beating to the sound of the windshield wipers. The rain soon ended, and by nightfall that unforgettable Friday, I saw the Gateway Arch in St. Louis, Missouri, as I crossed the Mississippi River. I spent the night alone in a Howard Johnsons in downtown St. Louis, feeling like I was just learning to walk. Not caring where, just walking and walking and walking, holding on to no one.

It was the time of Good Vibrations, California Dreamin', Mustang Sally, Drive My Car, and Like a Rolling Stone. Through the city of Joplin I thought of Janis. Behind me the Ozarks, like a formidable wall, rose between me and the winter I had known. Before me Route 66 extended through the open plains of Oklahoma. Far ahead the September heat danced over the tarmac, the radio blared out the windows into unimaginable distance and I sang into that distance and the uncharted sky.

I took my time getting to California. There were so many things I had never even imagined: petrified forests, two headed snakes and frogs, meteor craters, and most of all the Grand Canyon. On Route 180 past Valle, the earth changed from two dimensions into the seemingly infinite depths. I had to pull off. My eyes filled with tears at the majesty before me, and I sat at the South Rim for hours as the sun slowly descended. Shadow and light played against the mile-high walls of that chasm, brushed in sienna, lavender, and beryl. A mist settled over the far end of the canyon and I saw the aqueous blue of the Colorado River far below, its chiseling current concealed in distance. Over this scene, the moon now hovered, understated and diminished, like a shimmery pearl in a dark vast ocean.

Nothing in my life had prepared me for the culture shock of California. Everything about it seemed limitless from the Mojave Desert to the Pacific Ocean, to the lights of Los Angeles at night, as if the stars had fallen and tumbled over the horizon.

Many answers were there about what I dreamed it would be like, except one. *Who are you?*

Where was the answer for me to find? In what mirror? I pursued an acting career. Was it to lose myself in the fiction of characters, the anesthesia of fame and wealth, entranced by experimentation and adventure? Under the warm blanket of Santa Ana Winds the Pacific Ocean held testaments, writhing in the waters of receding tides, leaving the future buried in the sand. Evening suns interred on horizons. I wandered in California for seven years, through cities, mountains and valleys, rivers and lakes, and the very real dark tunnels of love, but found nothing there—only reasons to leave.

## Photograph of a Poem

The parallel lines may be green,
but you do not yet know the poem
so it is difficult to be certain.

Between the lines could be rows
of dark, loamy soil, like tanned fingers,
seen through a possibly cloudless sky.

*Was the sky blue—not one cloud?*

The sky could not be seen, but it was blue
and all around the hot, dry day
clouds could not be found over land and trees.

*There were trees—the green lines?*
*Describe the trees. Is there a plane?*

The poem has no plane, but, yes, trees
possibly, a fragrance from somewhere,
intoxicating like a woman's hair,

black like a raven soaring over verdant groves,
full with ripened fruit, her fingers brown
around the complicated long lens,
seeing the poem through a cloudless sky.

*What are the groves? Are they the woman?*
*Is the loam her brown fingers? Is this*
*a love poem, and what are the trees?*
*Name the ripened fruit.*

Picture oranges on the trees. See only
the fruit, the woman's hair and delicate
brown fingers, reaching.

The poem expands beyond its boundaries.
Intoxicating, heavy air carries us like clouds.
The poem circles like a raven,
but there is no plane.

## Birds in Home Depot—December

They sing, staccato notes:
statements that could be,
*queer tree, queer tree...*

Sometimes I see them
brown dots on a brown beam.

No easy nest here,
the spruce branches broken,
straw sequestered tight in brooms
wrapped in cellophane,

except for the threadbare Fall
scarecrow, braced firmly
among the colored corn stalks
and baskets of stippled gourds.

I want them to see the irony
under the steel beams
where they hop and fly, searching—
the fragments of a home
imagined new, repaired, changed.

In the garden center, a sparrow
contemplates the crocus bulbs,
huddled on shelves, awaiting Spring,
under the canopy that lets
in the sky and cool air.

I've wandered these aisles,
like today with my scribbled list,
unable to find a pin for a screen
door, a number four brass screw
for a fan, a summer breeze.

What does that weaver know,
I wonder, as he tugs at browned
lily leaves and with a torn fragment flies
out the wide opened doors.

## Before the Rain

A carmine sky inclined
itself against the bulk
of night while you slept.

Speckled doves coo
on clutched wires,
as though the prairie
was comprised of marionettes,
staged in a tented fete,
the footlights of morning
kindled over the horizon.

From an updraft a dry tongue
screams on a hyphen of wings
spread over the rising wind.

The cactus with its bruised pears
and cloistered blooms
pricks at the rivers
raging in the air
behind the shifting
curtain of coming day,
prepared in silence,
for a moment not yet here,
from gathered oceans,
breath and tarn,
utterance and tear.

## Tree Frog

You repeat like the grasses and the reeds
and hide in the future of inevitable evening.

You soothe me into dreams adrift toward morning
and reveal yourself in chalices of seclusion.

You speak in tongues
and you jazz like nobody's business.

You harmonize with silence and your voice
fills the sad spaces left by the owl and loon.

Your song is brighter than moonlight, your song
floats on the waters' breathing.

Your spirit rises in the rubbing of wet shoes
and I do not remember first hearing you,

because I have never not loved you;
I carry your chant in the crevasses of my words.

I have broken apart the din of cities to hear you
and no longer doubt that music is a found thing.

You make me remember the holiness of repetition
and the mysteries of the world.

You teach me the lightness of not knowing,
as I stumble in darkness with open eyes.

You cannot be found by searching,
and because the bough does not feel your burden,

the earth has embraced you in its infinite branches.
The last chord that will carry me away shall be yours

## Moonlight Sonata

Countess Giulietta, for you the gentle
ruminations came in simple chords,
that rose and rose again in questions.

You and he in midnight air, wordlessly,
secretly, arm in arm, he in stride
and you reticent, corset and train.

Did Rellstab name it from a vision
in Lucerne? Or was *Quasi Una Fantasia*
for you, the love and dream.

What garden, walked in moonlight?
What visions came so hauntingly, silently,
beautifully, like the quiet wings of night birds

that nested in the strings, the grain of wood
that felt his ear against its subtle breathing,
when they sang of black fleeing into black.

His lamentation turned to prayer, lifting
to the night sky, descending to despair,
demanding the air deliver its motion.

He returned, Giulietta, to that garden,
in its darkest paces, resolved that Schiller's Joy,
the Ninth be bound within him,

bound in silence, but for the unbearable sound of faces.

## Horse Sense

Pisanello, the medalist,
laid and combed his bristle
in the manes of stallions.

He carved out of the night sky
its brilliance to capture in repose
a unicorn, and for the princess Cecilia
her life's lost moonlight.

With horses, lithe and muscled
as the finest in Milan,
at auction in Bologna for the Duke,
it was strange to see an artist
bidding wise.

To put him off they said,
it's clear you are no horse trader.
Oh! said he, and clearly
I can see
you've never painted them.

## Who Stole the Tarts?

Not the breakfast cake,
but something hidden
within us to make us rise.

Like in the streets, a face
from out of the shadows
provides for some, a crutch of flesh;

or a ghost orchid on a dark tree,
where a new swamp, fetid and tall,
grows 'round a sweet purchase.

Wonderland, the dream tells you
the sidewalks are wide enough
for promises, and long enough to take you home.

So why are these familiar rooms
different than before? And these grapes
are without their ominous wince.

Alice says the dream and the eye are one,
evil lives, but reflection beckons us, even
though the looking glass is full of tears.

# VI • Colorado, Texas, Ohio, North Carolina

After a brief winter stay in Boulder, Colorado, I drove east to Houston, Texas and began college studies in biology at the University of St. Thomas. But my first literature professor, Joy Wilson, convinced me to write and switch my major. I was naïve about reading and literature. In class I felt like a sailor lost at sea. There, in my twenty-sixth year of life, I knew nothing about studying. I had read a few books, but stopped where the words lay and walked over each line like stepping stones to an end. My first required essay was a report on the novel by Kurt Vonnegut, *Slaughterhouse Five*. Tortured for the week prior to the due date I came up with nothing. On the weekend before the Monday class, I just wrote how I felt while reading the novel. When I was handed the graded paper with an *A*, Joy Wilson mouthed the words, "You write very well." As I was leaving the room she asked me to stop by her office that afternoon. I suppose my future was set in that meeting, and in the encouragement of several other professors who commented positively on my writing.

I finished two years at the University of St. Thomas, and decided to leave Houston. I didn't like the humid weather, nor the atmosphere of such a large city. One night I drove my motorcycle, surrounded by books, into a U-Haul trailer, and I drove east on the same road where once I rambled west.

For the second time in my life I returned to Ohio, to attend Denison University where I graduated with high honors in Anthropology and English Literature. After graduation I drove towing my books and meager possessions to Chapel Hill, NC to attend graduate school in Cultural Anthropology. After not being accepted three times, I took a position as an editor for an educational research firm, and from there a freelance technical writer. I moved once again seventeen miles south of Chapel Hill to a small town, founded by Quakers, called Snow Camp. I lived there on three-hundred and fifty acres for twenty years. The seasons of Columbus, Spain, and California faded, leaving seeds that would flourish in me for the remainder of my life. My house was a sixty-five year old farm house on Bethel South Fork Road. It was heated by a large wood stove. There were walls of double-hung windows six feet high and three feet wide that opened to country sides that entered me the way the dew of mornings enter the air of the day. To the east was a short rock wall and hundreds of iris along a large pond. Across the road was another pond. I could watch the kingfishers dive for their meals. Each night sleep came to me with a serenade of tree frogs, bullfrogs, and crickets. Something I miss to this day. In the back of the house was a canning room with a porcelain sink and countertop, all surrounded by casement windows and screens.

In my tenth year in Snow Camp, I rescued a dog named Molly. She was a German Shepherd that was twenty percent wolf. To say the least, she was majestic and incredibly smart. My walks in the woods were enhanced by her presence. I took her everywhere I went. She especially loved trips to the mountains where she would sit quietly while I fished for trout. Molly loved sleeping in a tent, and behaved cautiously when bears and other critters scrounged the campsite in the dead of night.

Not too far down the road from my house was an immense Southern Magnolia that was well over one-hundred years old. I would sit inside its branches, imagining it was a church—the flowers releasing an ambient fragrance over its prodigious grotto. Across from my house was a stand of pine trees that would allow me to get lost if I chose to. A front porch swing provided hours of gentle rocking while listening and feeling the breezes through the trees. From there I could see timothy in the field beyond sway and change hues in what seemed like visual symphony. The field beyond an apple orchard bore a rainbow of morning glories every year, defying any of the worst winters I endured. It was a paradise to live there for so long.

My years in Snow Camp, North Carolina, permanently changed me from the self-seeking boy who ventured to California looking for answers to the wrong questions, ignoring every sign I was given toward a true path. Finally, seeking work as a technical writer, I moved to Saint Petersburg, Florida.

## Leaving Carolina

Birds like black smoke rise
from Autumn's fire. Cool nights
push fescue from its roots,
and wiregrass hunkers down
under the brown and amber past.

Now I must leave.
The Jonquils here are sleeping fast,
yet gold lies all around,
to be, rather than to seem,
a sign that first green too may last.

My boot print leaves no trace
in your mountain streams. Look
there in a trout's face for me,
or on a patch of tended ground
where rue grows with the columbine.

What led me here I cannot say
for sure, nor say what kept me here
was ever meant to be,
but I know my heart was blue
long before I saw your skies.

# Even When

your porch is framed
with snow, fallen
in belvederes
along the rails,
the stairs in shocks
of delicate obstruction,
where my progress
fails in quiet awe—

even then,
though the baffles
of November
come between us,
I hear your song,
released with sweet abandon,
a promise for
my wintered soul.

## Grounded

I sift the soil between my hands,
then part the earth and plant a seed.
How marvelous these mounds and bands
will bring us everything we need.

The rains are late, and as I weed,
I sift the soil between my hands
and pack it down. So light, the seed
may wash away, from clay and sand.

But comes the rain and soaks the land.
By May the tender sprouts are freed,
I sift the soil between my hands,
and help direct them where they lead.

Days grow short, the rows are screed.
Beets are pickled, beans are canned.
Winter snows that Spring succeed.
I sift the cold between my hands.

# Stopping By the Farming Pavilion

*after Robert Frost*

The wheat as seed is dry yet slides,
like river water, side on side.
Grown pale with beards bide these old men
who wear their wrinkled brows with pride.

Like vibrant souls they wait for when
the earth will make them green again—
strong and supple in the breeze,
though heavy in their heads by then.

It's not so strange a poet sees
his human life portrayed in these
exuberant and golden grains,
and hopes within in his reveries.

Divergent is our fruited plain,
some fertile, while the rest need rain.
So many things we can't explain.
So many things we can't explain.

## VII • Florida Again

In Saint Petersburg, I moved into a house that stood at the edge of Coffeepot Bayou, a place beyond time at the end of Thirtieth Ave. North. The brick boulevard along the seawall meandered in front of old Florida plantation style mansions having huge yards landscaped with Bird of Paradise, peonies the size of tea saucers, the discordant bloom of blue hydrangea, and the relic of Spanish bayonet. A sun-speckled passage was lined with the narrow gills of Banyan trees, palms of all kinds, and ancient live Oaks from before the discovery of Florida, trees with their impossibly long and sweeping limbs festooned in moss, dangling down and swayed to the slightest breeze. Over the seawall, out in the bayou were small islands of Mangrove pied with perched egrets. Occasionally, one or two would spread their wings in a brief flight, like white clouds brushed by a high wind, then settle back elsewhere into the mound of tangled branches. Coffeepot Bayou suited Molly and I just fine.

Five months after we moved to Coffeepot Bayou, Molly succumbed to kidney failure. She was half the reason I chose the house we lived in and now there were no more morning and evening walks along the seawall and the unleashed freedom of Dog Beach, adjacent to the park. At first, in the stupor of a rough day at work, when I would forget, the absence of her tail thumping the floor as I came through the door was unbearable; there was an open pit where a living room once held her rejuvenating welcome each day; the elixir of love that everyday would instantly lift all my burdens was no longer there.

Continuing to live in that house was agonizing. Molly was

gone and soon after her death my house was robbed. It seemed any peace I had mustered was gone as well. Occasionally. the police reported on their progress with the robberies occurring in my neighborhood, which was only a reminder of my loss. The thieves had taken Molly's ashes, why I do not know, but the investigators seemed to place a great deal of weight on them and where Molly was cremated. I began looking for another place to live. It was difficult to find a place in a large city after living in Snow Camp for so long. I did not want to hear road noise. I did not want my window view to be a parking lot. I also needed to consider the distance I would have to travel to work. Main access roads in Saint Petersburg were heavily traveled.

At the end of that year, I moved to an apartment. It was a serene home with a balcony that overlooked an expanse of trees that stretched into a horizon, beyond which lay Tampa Bay. The new place was a sanctuary for me, allowing me to recover from several years of turmoil in my life. My father had died of Alzheimer's just before I moved. I flew to Ohio for the funeral. We were never very close, but there it seems I began the years-long search for how it was I loved him in the strange way I loved him. I began to see him as the artist he was, and the pain he must have felt leaving his stained glass work and his beloved workshop behind our house on Medary Ave. when I was a boy.

When the weather permitted, I opened the French doors to my apartment, and at night let in the calls of whippoorwills orchestrated, it seemed, with wind-swept sounds from the pines, oaks, palms, and, on the fragrance of a salt breeze, the pattering of large round leaves of the mangroves from the islands in the bayou. Mornings, the songs of Redwing Blackbirds, Mockingbirds and gulls drifted through the open doors as I wrote in what had become a peaceful meditation.

Almost a year later, one Saturday in my apartment, I received a call from the St. Petersburg police department. The person on the call said they may have recovered Molly's remains, and requested that I come to the station downtown. As I drove, I began wondering if other items had been recovered. Recovering Molly's ashes meant I could do what I had always hoped and release them in the mountains that she loved.

At the station an officer escorted me to a room with tables covered with white paper. "These are items recovered in a house in Five Points. We have the urn with your dog's remains. You can look on the tables for any other items that are yours. Let us know and we'll collect them for you. We think a lot of what was stolen has been sold at pawn shops and we're working on recovering as many of those items as possible."

I walked and paused, walked and paused along the row of tables, astounded at the quantity of personal items that had been grouped together. It was sad. There were photos in frames of families, young and old, weddings, graduations, smiling, laughing clusters of people forever happy in those brief moments, far from whatever had happened since, far from the indifferent hands that removed them to a vacant and dark house away from the wellspring to which they belonged.

There were other people walking and pausing with me. Some were crying as they discovered wedding rings, lockets, heirlooms. And there were those who had stopped what they were doing, or cancelled their Saturday routines and rushed here with hope, only to find nothing.

At the last table, I turned to walk back to the office and get Molly's urn, when I saw a small bronze figurine of a German

Shepherd, sitting proud, its ears perked. A childhood poem by Eugene Field drifted into my mind, "The little toy dog is covered with dust…," and then I realized it was *my* figurine. I had purchased it years ago at an antique store. Now tears came. There was no guitar, no TV or stereo, but there was this time-darkened bronze dog that symbolized all the years of unparalleled love and affection that had been mine to receive and give. I recovered Molly's ashes and the figurine and went home.

The police discovered the house full of stolen items when a neighbor complained of a barking and whining dog. When they opened the door there was no dog. There were rooms packed with the personal belongings of households around Coffeepot Bayou. And there was a beige urn. In that urn was a bag of ashes with a small metal ID: Molly 31556—Rainbow Bridge. The police contacted the cemetery and found my name associated with Molly's ashes. This connected the thieves directly to the robberies. *The St. Petersburg Times* ran a half page story about the robberies and how the thieves were apprehended. Molly got her name in the paper and was the star of the story. "Remarkable Dog Apprehends Thieves Even After Death" read the headline.

I lived in that place until I met Carol, the love of my life, and her two daughters Abby and Allison. After a year I moved into Carol's townhouse in Treasure Island, Florida. We were married in Jamaica soon after. There remained yet journeys we would take, and we took them together: to the mountains of Eureka Springs, Arkansas, and the Hill Country of central Texas, where we are today. I'm sure there will be other stories to come, stories resting in twenty-two years of marriage.

# On Treasure Island

*for Carol*

If September hadn't come,
to wake us from our past,
whose sunflower would be
the one I gave to you?

The rain that dropped our secrets
in the evening air
may have let them fall
into a deep and silent sea,
to never find a shore.

We are like two shells found
along the sand, pearl colored
open twists, winsomely turned
inside, where we have listened
to each others' ocean calling.

# What I Share with the Rain

*for Molly*

hides in dog simplicity—
her tongue slapping at backwater,
no bowl and, after rain, the puddles
from the weight of wheels,
like mine she feared at first,
as if she knew something, as we do often:
that death is bound to life
in unexpected ways:

a ride, head out the window, ears flapping
(the wind made breathing easy),

and later, my voice from which she gained
a grace for shots and vets,
like the one I endured with her,
completing what began years ago,
her rescue too late, her drinking
the rain that lifted the green pearls
wheels had left in their swales.

**Fortunes**

When we moved they were lost,
the fortunes I had saved
that seemed to mean something.

"Suppose you get what you want,"
read the first one; I taped it to the wall,
then each new one of significance
under that, like a ladder leading to the first.

There is no one here who knows me.
The trees on the manicured streets are small and bare,
there are no songs in the branches.

Someone brought cookies; rang the bell,
as I was digging in boxes for the small
clip that held them tightly—the small,
flags of inspiration, steps I freed from their brittle shells.

## SRV in the Parking Lot At the Quick Stop

No traffic,
light coming up
with the radio—
Lenny's here, really here.

Do you cry
when you play her,
where the fret moves into the music box
I dance inside,
sometimes I risk it driving—
bow my head and shake
where the clear notes sound tenor up the neck,
bass in a tin can like a kick
oh my!

Margarine for my sweetheart, butter me—
whiskey's too early, but those cigarettes
sleep in my heart like a snare vibrating
in the red rising sky like it's all I've got left.

Here now, people come and go,
Lenny loud low, lingering me in the parking lot—

I can't leave you like this radio,
staring into the space behind the world,
fingers walking like these vagabond birds—
not for sweet love or even neat coffee.

## Slipper

*for Carol*

Watching your feet traipse the shoreline sand
that forms itself for a moment like a slipper, disappearing
in the ocean's wet arc following you, I
know what happens next, the water deepens
around us as we walk, our ankles draped in the last
    wave's wet lace,
each step now more a memory beyond the force of tides
than something we do to make our way
in occult and fleeting shoes,
cobbled from a thousand years—you and I
into the brackish air, into the crush of shells.

# After Dreams

*for Carol*

In the mornings as sleep leaves us slowly,
we are one body, like the waters of the oceans.

Your fragrance enters me the way light entwined
itself into the fabric of night and while we slept

found its way through louvers and now lies unseen
in the curl of yesterday's tossed clothes.

Even before my eyes open to the room
as we had left it, I am listening to the first birds,

like sailors, long at sea, listen for the gulls.
I do not look into the distance of the room,

I wait for the slender purl of your voice,
like morning waves breaking softly on a new shore.

# Please Stay

*for Carol*

I heard you singing in the next room,
sporadic—a disordered tune,
and behind the notes, the water ran,
the grace of clinking plates, your hands
warm water soothed, and thus the tune.

Through open windows a sort of choir
attended you and it seemed conspired
to fill each space, like time with sand.
I heard you singing

and knew that pain might stop you soon,
slant your peace toward gloom,
but for now please stay in whatever land
your song exists, like some magic wand
transported you, where in some soothing room
I heard you singing.

## Wedding Wish

*for Abby and Nick, July 6, 2014*

Now you know the way
love enters you,

everything stringed
and vibrant, singing.

May love always sound
in you, even in the absence of words,

the way silk ripples
on a windless day.

# Hearts

*for Ally and Clint, December 13, 2014*

Love has no time for time,
no place decreed to meet us,
nor perfect moment to appear;
it is most like the silent stars
that from a deep eternity
arrive each night like angels of grace.

Love is an open space,
without a door, it's what we are.

We do not create love. It is here
before us, in the poetry of clouds,
in the boughs of trees it whispers, and weaves
its voice through the throats of canyons.

The earth is moving, a quiet, gentle heart,
rocking ever slowly in a breast of sky,
and with its colors, white and blue,
with its arms of day and night,
may it bless you both,
forever giving peace to you.

# Window

Outside, the Maple seeds turn as they fall,
turn in complex spirals from their branches.

*Sleep, baby, as I rock,* as the maple sways
in the gusts of air, shaking loose its twirling birds.

I have been you, wrapped warm near a forgotten pane,
seasons rushing, now it seems, through dresses, shoes,

cap and veil, the leaves rolling behind my eyes,
over Fall lawns, then buried under flawless snows.

What shapes and sounds conspire to bring you dreams,
before you discover the scattering force of the world?

There will be a morning when you rise and find a road away
from me, my love left pressed like maple leaves in a book.

Years will pass in pages I write to keep you
in my heart; the years will turn in orbits near and far.

For now, by this window, I hold you, your touch
like the small fingers of the rain—beyond us,
the leaves, and the indifferent arms of the wind.

## Still Life

*for my Father*

I remember saying my last "Our Father,"
you dead, arced with flower sprays,
daylight pushed through the stained glass, brushed
itself across white lilies like a canvas of Klee's.

*Man's time dissolves in ashes,* I repeated,
as the sun and the clouds conspired to make
a red pulse over a cross of carnations
and through the veins of the marble floor.

No one planned the wild buttercups in that field.
I brought no bouquet, nor did I kneel, but lay
down in your golden days and painted you to mind,
relieved of all your hidden colors.

# Mirror

I see my father's eyes,
now blue and calm—
the river has reached the sea—
as if he were at last happy,
with his life, his children grown
out of their angst, into the world.

When he laughs, his face glows,
unrecognizable at first,
no hesitation, the lines of his mouth
know easily where to go.

There is no fear, his brow is smooth,
but it is his face
and in its shadow parts, fierceness
hides, a beast from an old dream.

Back to the eyes, they are kind
and deep with joy and tears.
Before there was no memory of quiet
woods, the beautiful energy of waves
breaking themselves over rocks into pools,
a larger love learned by loving.

One final thing before the light is gone—
I love this face, even though it's one
I feared so long. You've changed
because of me. I have forgiven you.

## A Kind of Sleep

Dreamlessness is the shadows passing noiselessly
from trees, on tiptoes across the grass, past the window.

Here, between two worlds, the pearl turns on its chain,
becomes the bluish moon that waits throughout the day
to find its place on the dark neck of starless evening.

Of what do you not dream, when you do not dream?
Distance says night is where we live. At the end of day
light leaves its unraveling, like seasons
on the lawn, and there is enough to keep this attic
alive with the pulse of things struggling in fresh webs.

I come here among forgotten patches, the quilting frame,
with its labyrinth of ties, shirts and dresses, triangles
and squares holding fast to their distinctions, though cut
and sorted in their places. I seek to understand the story
of our life in this house from the past hung on its bones
in dark exhibits: lightless lanterns with withered wicks,
empty packs and creels, and placeless, faceless frames.
It is a placid rendering, a dim soul recalled in dust
and the spare voice of heartwood settling on a nail.

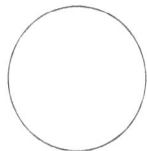

## Also from T. S. Poetry Press

*Earth Song: A Nature Poems Experience,* editor Sara Barkat

I am so grateful for this collection of poems. So many of my poetry heroes are in this book—Gerard Manley Hopkins and Robert Frost, Jane Hirshfield, Wendell Berry, Li-Young Lee, Pablo Neruda, Tomas Tranströmer—such a powerful gathering of voices that span centuries and continents.

—Rosemerry Wahtola Trommer, poet, winner of the Halcyon Prize and finalist for the Able Muse Book Award

*How to Read a Poem: Based on the Billy Collins Poem "Introduction to Poetry",* by Tania Runyan

No reader, experienced or new to reading poems, will want to miss this winsome and surprising way into the rich, wonderful conversations that poetry makes possible.

—David Wright, Assistant Professor of English at Monmouth College, IL

"I absolutely love this book. *Under the Pearl Moon* is more than a collection of masterful poems; it is a chronicle of a well-lived life. Weaving prose pieces with poetry, Rick Maxson skillfully creates a rich personal mythology of geography and memory—from the 1950s to present day, from growing up in a Craftsman home in Columbus, Ohio, to adult life in rural romantic North Carolina, and then on to Florida, where he discovers the love of his life. His paradise may in fact be along North Carolina's Eno River where he would 'so quietly live / among the particles of light and air,' and yet his poem, 'Tree Frog,' encapsulates the compelling, grand theme of the collection: 'You make me remember...the mysteries of the world...as I stumble in darkness with open eyes.'"

—Dave Malone, author of eight poetry collections, including *O: Love Poems from the Ozarks* and *Tornado Drill*

"Rick Maxson's poems—interspersed with brief personal essays bridging the geographical and psychic residencies of his life—sing with birds living inside a Home Depot, scintillate with 'solder stars' from a father's glass workshop, and stick to our fingers like the powdery binding of a decaying book of fairy tales. In the sensory intricacies of Maxson's language, we find a poetry so personal, so singularly woven with the memories of a life lived reflectively, that we can't help but find our own stories in the pages. Reading these poems is like basking in shared moonlight."

--Tania Runyan, author of *How to Write a Poem*, *How to Read a Poem*, *How to Write a Form Poem*

"You can read this utterly charming book of poems for its lifetime of places—Ohio, Spain, California, Colorado, Texas, North Carolina—even though the poet says there may be 'nothing there, only reasons to leave.' You can see the world through the eyes of a boy 'living in mystery fashioned by hapless adults,' where one might think, 'There is no one here that knows me.' You can also read *Under the Pearl Moon* as a paean to friends and family—a father who made windows, a mother 'who seemed to get whatever she wanted,' an uncle, sister, lover like 'shells found along the sand.' Or you can just ponder all the memorable lines and images along the way: 'Shoes with winter in their folds,' a refrigerator 'as close to food as words can come,' the sound of a treefrog that 'fills the sad spaces left by the owl and loon.' Whatever way you read this personable, thoughtful book, you will find, as the poet says, 'everything stringed and vibrant, singing.'"

—Jack Cooper, author of *Across My Silence*

"In lines full of music and pleasure and longing, Rick Maxson plots the rivers of his life, offering glimpses of love and hardship, of the working-class neighborhood where he spent his boyhood, of his travels and travails, his parents' desires and desperation, and his own path into a life rich with change. By making art of memory, he reminds us that we are 'sounds living for a moment, each one / disappearing into the next, / then each one gone.'"

—Todd Davis, author of *Coffin Honey* and *Native Species*

"'No place is a place until it's found its poet,' said Wallace Stegner, and in *Under the Pearl Moon*, Richard Maxson brings several places into their fullness, exploring them through memory, relationship, rejection, and layer on layer of wonder and questioning. These poems, each with jewel-like detail, help to tell a story of longing, leaving, return, and promise."

—Rosemerry Wahtola Trommer, author of *All the Honey* and host of The Poetic Path

"This rich collection marries memoir and poetry as Maxson seeks to understand the story of his life. Lyrical prose separates the sections, adding historical and geographic context to the reflective poems that follow. Moving across the U.S. and overseas proved traumatic *and* exciting to both the young and adult Maxson, and those experiences inform his writing. I especially enjoyed poems about his wife: 'I wait for the slender purl of your voice,' and about his father: 'the beautiful energy of waves / breaking themselves over rocks into pools, / a larger love learned by loving.'"

—Karen Paul Holmes, winner of the 2023 Lascaux Poetry Prize and author of *No Such Thing as Distance*

T. S. Poetry Press titles are available online in e-book and print editions. Print editions also available through Ingram.

tspoetry.com